1. The eyes of the Fleet in Nelson's day were his frigates; today, the eyes of the RN are slightly higher, but the frigates still play an important role. They are charged with patrol of the oceans in peacetime and the anti-submarine defence of groups in wartime; in addition, frigates would make up Surface Action Groups (SAG). In this photograph, taken in the English Channel, the Type 42 destroyer *Liverpool* (left) is commencing a jackstay transfer with the *Leander* Class frigate *Apollo*; in the background are *Alacrity* (a Type 21) and *Ariadne* (another *Leander*). (RN)

Warships Illustrated No 1

The ROYAL NAVY
in the 1980s
Volume I PAUL BEAVER

ARMS AND ARMOUR PRESS

Introduction

Published in 1985 by Arms and Armour Press,
2–6 Hampstead High Street, London NW3 1QQ.

Distributed in the United States by
Sterling Publishing Co. Inc., 2 Park Avenue,
New York, N.Y. 10016.

British Library Cataloguing in Publication Data:
Beaver, Paul
The Royal Navy in the 1980's. – (Warships
illustrated; no. 1)
1. Great Britain. *Royal Navy*   2. Warships
– Great Britain
I. Title   II. Series
623.8'25'0941   VA454
ISBN 0-85368-713-7

Editing, design and artwork by Roger Chesneau.
Typesetting by Typesetters (Birmingham) Ltd.
Printed in Italy by Tipolitografia G. Canale
& C. S.p.A., Turin, in association with Keats
European Ltd.

The 1980s are proving to be one of the most interesting periods in the postwar history of the Royal Navy, for not only have British maritime forces fought a 'war' some 8,000 miles from home ports (and Out of the NATO Area at that) but re-equipment with high technology systems is giving it the greatest capability ever. In terms of numbers of ships the RN is still in the top five 'blue water' navies; in terms of operational effectiveness and training, it must rank as top of the league. This picture album is a compilation of illustrations showing the way in which the Royal Navy is moving in the last quarter of the century, particularly from the point of view of equipment and of modifications to warship designs. With the continued presence of British warships off the Falkland Islands and the fact that at the time of writing Argentina has yet to sign a peace agreement, it has not been possible to go into too great detail, but the reader will be able to understand the basic philosophy behind the improvements in close-range weapons and specialist sensors.

Although anti-submarine warfare has always been important to the RN for the last forty years, the growing importance of the submarine itself has not been overlooked: Britain's independent deterrent force is carried by submarines, and the main counter-force to Soviet SSBNs lies with the new classes of fleet submarines, all nuclear-propelled. I have also tried to emphasize the work carried out in direct support of the 'Grey Funnel Line' by the auxiliary services, particularly the Royal Fleet Auxiliary Service. They have a maxim: 'RN sails courtesy RFA'.

In the middle of the 1980s, it seems that the Royal Navy is about to go through yet another cutting session, and projects which should be brought forward, especially with the increased Out of Area operations, will be shelved, postponed or even abandoned. Politicians would be wise to note that despite Britain's friendship with the United States and its membership of the European Community, it is a maritime nation. The British people should always be able to say 'Rule Britannia' with justifiable pride.

In obtaining many of the illustrations, I have received considerable assistance from the Royal Navy itself, especially the various Command PROs, the office of CINCFLEET (Commander-in-Chief Fleet) and CINCNAVHOME (Commander-in-Chief Naval Home Command), as well as from various ships and establishments and from the Fleet Photographic Unit. To them, I am most grateful, and must note that all RN and ships' pictures are British Crown Copyright.

Paul Beaver

◀2
2. The Polaris submarines, although nuclear-propelled, have auxiliary diesel generators for use when the reactor is 'cold', as in this picture of *Repulse* returning to Faslane. The Polaris missiles (sixteen Type A3 are carried) are stored in silos aft of the fin, and the 'R-boats' also have provision forward for Mk. 24 and perhaps Spearfish torpedoes. Note the after escape hatch with the special markings for the Deep Submergence Rescue Vehicle (DSRV). (HMS *Neptune*)

▲3 ▼4

5▲

3. The largest British warships built since the Second World War – the three *Invincible* Class aircraft carriers – have entered service during the 1980s. They were originally designated 'through-deck cruisers' to avoid the anti-carrier feeling in Parliament and the Civil Service, but the decision to buy the Sea Harrier FRS. 1 fighter changed the official designation, first to 'anti-submarine carrier' and later to 'light aircraft carrier'. The first of the class, *Invincible* (RO5), shows the characteristic 'ski-jump' bow ramp, on which a Sea Harrier is ranged. (HMS *Invincible*)

4. In wartime the *Invincibles* would act as command ships for British anti-submarine groups operating in the North Atlantic, and the ability of these 19,500-ton vessels to remain at sea with their air groups of about ten Sea King HAS.5/AEW.2 helicopters and six Sea Harriers is of paramount importance to NATO. Trials have recently been carried out to improve the possible choices for replenishment, and one of the earliest of these is illustrated here – the first ever beam RAS (replenishment at sea) with a merchant tanker, in this case *British Tamar*. The recipient is the second *Invincible* Class carrier *Illustrious*, operating in the Atlantic during May 1984. (HMS *Illustrious*)

5. The Royal Navy is an integrated part of the NATO alliance and as such often exercises with other members, particularly the US Navy, although the occasion here is rather unusual because the British warships, *Invincible* and *Rothesay*, are operating 'out of area', in the Indian Ocean. The US ships are *Ranger* (CV-61) and *Fife* (DD-991), and the photograph was taken during the 1983–84 Group Deployment to the Far East. (P.O. (Phot) O'Brien/HMS *Invincible*)

6. The aim of the *Invincible* Class is to take to sea a 'large number of anti-submarine warfare helicopters', which during the 1980s means the Westland Sea King HAS.5 and in the 1990s might mean the EH.101 now under development. The class was designed without provision for short take-off and vertical landing (STOVL) fighters, but, during building, *Invincible* received a 7° 'ski-jump' to increase the operational ability of the Sea Harrier. This photograph of *Invincible* was taken in July 1984, after the carrier had completed repairs at Devonport to rectify a faulty propeller and shaft, and shows a Sea King HAS.2 recovering to Spot 3 on the flight deck. (P.O. (Phot) Kent/HMS *Invincible*)

◄6

▲7

7. The main self-defence weapon of the *Invincible*s is the Sea Dart medium-range anti-aircraft and anti-surface missile system. The launcher is positioned forward of the flight deck and has meant that the deck's centreline has had to be offset ½° in order to accommodate the 'ski-jump' as well. During the Falklands conflict, the Sea Dart proved to be a versatile missile although the Admiralty was concerned that it was not sufficient to protect the carrier close-in. On returning to the UK, *Invincible* was fitted with extra 20mm Oerlikon cannon and with countermeasures launchers. (HMS *Illustrious*)

8. Air defence is also provided for the carriers by the BAe Sea Harrier FRS.1, which equips 800 (*Illustrious*) and 801 Sqns. (*Invincible*). The aircraft's main armament consists of the AIM-9L Sidewinder missile, four of which may be carried, and two under-

fuselage 30mm Aden cannon pods. Operating from *Invincible* and *Hermes* during the South Atlantic campaign, April–June 1982, the Sea Harrier accounted for twenty Argentine aircraft with missiles and guns, plus three probables; six were lost, though none to aerial combat. (Fleet Photographic Unit)

9. The *Invincible*s are powered by four Rolls-Royce Marine Olympus gas turbines, developing 112,000 shaft horse power and giving the carriers a speed of at least 28kts. One interesting feature of the engines is that they can be changed whilst the ship is at sea, as demonstrated here by the Marine Engineering Department of *Illustrious*, May 1984. Using the hangar and aircraft lifts, the engines can be transferred to shore and new units taken aboard. (HMS *Illustrious*)

▼8

9▶

▲10

▲11 ▼12

13▲

10. Following experience in the South Atlantic, the decision was taken to arm the *Invincibles* with the Vulcan Phalanx 20mm Close-In Weapon System (CIWS). *Illustrious* was fitted with two units (the flight deck mounting is illustrated) during her final completion in June 1982, and *Invincible* was fitted on her return to the UK in September. The third ship of the class, *Ark Royal*, has received three Phalanx. (HMS *Illustrious*)

11. The Sea Harriers have also been modified in the light of the South Atlantic experience and will receive a further update in 1985–87. Initially, they were fitted to take larger auxiliary fuel tanks and new twin launchers for the Sidewinder air-to-air missile system, but further improvements will include new Ferranti radar and upgraded avionics, plus additions to the wings to improve the aircraft's already impressive manoeuvrability and fighting agility. This is one of

801 Sqn's aircraft, pictured on *Invincible*'s flight deck during the ship's visit to Fremantle.

12. In 1984 *Illustrious* again undertook trials with the Sea King airborne early warning (AEW) helicopter, which uses a powerful radar, Thorn EMI Searchwater, to search for and track possible enemy aircraft and missiles which would pose a threat to the carrier task group. It is envisaged that by 1988 three Sea King AEW.2s will be embarked in each *Invincible* Class carrier, and trials will be undertaken for them to go to sea in Royal Fleet Auxiliaries.

13. In this photograph, *Illustrious* is conducting full power and manoeuvring trials off Portugal during 'Autumn Train 1984'. Sea Harrier FRS.1s and Sea King HAS.5s (one of the latter in the 'grey whale' scheme introduced in 1984) are ranged on deck. (HMS *Illustrious*)

11

▲15 ▼16

14. (Previous spread) Immediately following Exercise 'Autumn Train 1984', the latest British aircraft carrier put to sea from her builder's yard on the Tyne. The fifth ship to bear the name, *Ark Royal* commissions in 1985 and has the benefit of many improvements as a result of the Falklands experience and of the general service use of her two predecessors. In this photograph she is shown with *Illustrious* (left) in the North Sea. The newer ship has a steeper 'ski-jump' and a port sponson for a third Phalanx CIWS; *Illustrious* is carrying the first of the 'grey whale' Sea Kings. (HMS *Illustrious*)

15. In the 1960s the decision was taken to cancel all plans for the Royal Navy to operate conventional, fixed-wing aircraft carriers after 1978. The programme to build a special class of guided missile destroyers to escort the new generation of aircraft carriers was also cancelled, but not before the first ship had been built – *Bristol*, the sole Type 82 destroyer. From 1972, she has been employed as a trials ship for the Sea Dart missile system (mounted abaft the superstructure) and the Ikara anti-submarine system (forward); *Bristol* also mounts a Vickers Mk. 8 4.5in gun. (Fleet Photographic Unit)

16. The *County* Class guided missile destroyers were designed to operate the Sea Slug medium-range anti-aircraft missile and the Seacat short-range AAM, and they were tasked with providing escort for carriers and amphibious groups, as well as carrying out police duties in the Far East and West Indies. The class is now considered 'manpower-intensive', and in 1985 only two remain in service, *Glamorgan* (illustrated) and *Fife*. *Kent* is a harbour training ship, *Hampshire* has been scrapped, *Antrim* and *Norfolk* were sold to Chile and *London* sold to Pakistan, and *Devonshire* was expended as a target for the new Sea Eagle missile system. (HMS *Osprey*)

17. Designed to meet the air defence needs of a task force, particularly that built around an aircraft carrier, the Type 42 destroyers, formerly called the *Sheffield* Class, are driven by a combination of Rolls-Royce Olympus and Tyne gas turbines, giving them speeds in excess of 30kts. Twelve ships have been ordered, for completion by 1986, and seven were in commission by the end of 1985; two (*Sheffield* and *Coventry*) were lost in 1982. This is *Birmingham* (D86), pictured as built in 1980. (Rolls-Royce)

18. Apart from the Westland Lynx HAS.2/3 helicopter, the main armament of the Type 42s is the Sea Dart area air defence missile system and the Vickers Mk. 8 4.5in gun. Here pictured aboard *Newcastle*, the Vickers gun is unmanned in action and is currently the largest-calibre weapon afloat with the Royal Navy. Also visible on deck is the emergency anchor, strapped to the bridge, and the bridge-top Type 909 radar for the Sea Dart system.

17▲   18▼

▲19
19. Generally accepted as being the most efficient navy in the world, the Royal Navy keeps its reputation by continual exercises and continuous evaluation. The ability to mount an operation 8,000 nautical miles from the nearest home port was demonstrated in 1982, and RN warships are often to be found operating away from home. *Liverpool* (D92), a Batch 2 Type 42, and the 'Broad-Beamed *Leander*' *Apollo* are seen exercising during a jackstay transfer.
20. Her normal North Atlantic paint scheme toned down for
▼20

operations in the South Atlantic, the Type 42 destroyer *Nottingham* (D91) shows her graceful lines. The major difference between the Batch 1 and Batch 2 ships of this class is shown externally by the latter's Type 1022 radar. This system, which also equips the *Invincible* Class carriers, is designed for air and surface search; the mainmast radar is Type 992, for surveillance and target indication, whilst the two Type 909 radars (in the radomes) are for targeting and controlling the Sea Dart. (Fleet Photographic Unit)

21▲

21. The Batch 1 and Batch 2 Type 42s suffered from a lack of internal space, especially for the weapons systems, and there was simply no room for growth. The last four ships, the Batch 3s, have therefore been lengthened and broadened to allow the CIWS and a Ship-launched Torpedo Weapons System (STWS) to be fitted. The design is also more seaworthy and has certain other modifications, including refinements to the Action Information Organization (AIO) which controls the ship in battle.

22. Following the experiences of the Falklands War, particularly the destruction of *Sheffield*, *Coventry*, *Ardent* and *Antelope*, the Royal Navy has undertaken a rapid upgrading of the close-in weapons of its escort ships. The destroyers and frigates were given extra 20mm and 30mm mountings amidships; one such weapon was the Oerlikon 20mm KAA cannon on the BMARC mounting, as illustrated here aboard *Manchester*.

22▼

23. A more powerful addition to the ship's short-range defences is the Oerlikon 30mm GCM-A03 twin mounting, placed on specially fitted sponsons amidships on 01 deck. The new close-range battery is well situated, but there are plans to improve the range- and direction-finding. Note the name given to *Manchester*'s port-side mounting.

24. In addition to the 30mm Oerlikon (seen here immediately after a practice shoot and with its crew still wearing anti-flash masks and gauntlets), *Manchester* is armed with the STWS ASW system. The STWS Mk. 32 uses the Mk. 44, Mk. 46 and Stingray lightweight torpedoes for short-range anti-submarine operations; all three types are wire-guided and can be carried by the ship's Lynx helicopter.

25. Not only is the Lynx helicopter capable of carrying anti-submarine torpedoes and depth bombs, but, without much effort, it can also deploy the Sea Skua air-to-surface missile. This weapon is especially useful against patrol craft and warships up to corvette size, enabling the parent ship to direct an attack against a small target at long range. *Southampton*'s Lynx is pictured here recovering aboard the destroyer, which is alongside at Portsmouth. Note that the helicopter is equipped with a magnetic anomaly detector (MAD) as an additional ASW sensor. (RN)

26. Despite the cessation of hostilities between Argentina and Great Britain in the South Atlantic, there has been, at the time of writing, no peace treaty. It has therefore been the task of the Royal Navy to keep a force in the South Atlantic in order to maintain the Exclusion Zone. Pictured leaving Portsmouth for 'down south' is *Newcastle* (D87), her new weaponry and shortage of sea boats (taken off to compensate for the extra topweight) very much in evidence. (RN)

▲23 ▼24

27. The United Kingdom's most important strategic weapon is the nuclear ballistic missile, Polaris, carried by four 'R' Class nuclear-propelled submarines; all four are based at Faslane (the Clyde submarine base) and form the 10th Submarine Squadron. These boats are seen on the surface only when setting out on patrol or returning to port: this is *Revenge*, returning to Faslane under a wintry Scottish sunset. (HMS *Gannet*)

28. Every several years, the 'R-boats' undertake a two-year refit at Rosyth naval base where they are modernized to ensure their continued ability to demonstrate a credible strategic deterrence force for the United Kingdom. In October 1984 *Repulse*, the second of the class to be commissioned, entered Rosyth for her third such refit. Of interest is the paying off pennant flying from the search periscope; note also the submarine's bell on the fin casing. (FOSNI/RN)

27▶

▼28

◀30

29. The backbone of the RN's submarine force is the nuclear-propelled fleet submarine (SSN), used as the primary naval anti-submarine weapon as well as to counter surface ship threats. The first of the type to be built with a British nuclear reactor was *Valiant* (S102), commissioned in 1966 and destined to go out of service some time after her twentieth birthday. On 'deck' in this photograph is the casing party, with the bridge watchkeepers, captain and navigator in the fin, and the boat is negotiating the difficult passage along the Clyde to the open sea. (HMS *Neptune*)

30. *Valiant* again, showing, immediately behind the Casing Officer (CASO), the French-designed passive sonar used for listening to other noise-makers; other sonar equipment has its sensors in the bow, below the trimline. The early British SSNs have their forward diving planes above their normal trimline when surfaced, as here, whilst later models have retractable planes. (HMS *Neptune*)

▲31

31. Part of the calendar for several of the Royal Navy's SSNs is an 85-day patrol which will include the South Atlantic. During this time, the only break for the crew will be a rendezvous in San Carlos Water with a supply ship. This is *Courageous*, on her last patrol before entering Devonport for refit, and of interest is the extended mast array – the search periscope (left) and the radio mast. (CINCFLEET)

32. One SSN has achieved special fame. The 4,900-ton (dived) submarine *Conqueror* was operational in the South Atlantic in 1982 and became the first SSN to be used in action when she sank the Argentine cruiser *General Belgrano*, which at the time was threatening the British Task Force. When she returned to Faslane she flew the 'Jolly Roger' and was given a special welcome. (RN)

33. The *Swiftsure* Class SSNs – this picture, taken in Gare Loch,

shows the name-ship – are deeper-diving and faster than the previous two classes; in addition, they have only five torpedo tubes, all forward, to reduce the number of openings in the pressure hull and thus improve diving ability. *Swiftsure* is shown being escorted from Faslane by the 'nuclear safety boat', the Royal Maritime Auxiliary Service tug *Labrador*. (HMS *Neptune*)

34. Nuclear-propelled submarines often make courtesy visits to British and European ports, which not only give the public an opportunity to see the Submarine Flotilla but also allow the boat's company some rest and recreation. Visiting Southampton in June 1983, *Sceptre* took part in the annual boat show at this south coast port. (Mike Lennon)

▼32

33▲   34▼

▲35

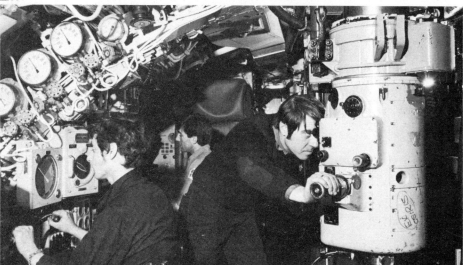

▲36 ▼37

35. The ship's control centre of the second *Trafalgar* Class fleet submarine *Turbulent* during a training dive in the Irish Sea. The position is manned for normal passage by a Petty Officer, who oversees two Leading Rates, one on the 'planes/rudder and the other controlling the diving and trim tanks. The photograph was taken from the Action Information Organization part of the Control Room; the large metal cylinder to the right is the attack periscope in the stowed position.

36. The control room of a conventional (diesel-electric powered) submarine is rather cramped, and the living conditions of those working in the boat's nerve centre could be considered restrictive. Two ratings are shown at the boat's controls and a Petty Officer has his eye to the search periscope in this posed photograph which was probably taken alongside or in the submarine trainer. (HMS *Dolphin*)

37. Manning the wheel of an SSN is rather like flying an aeroplane – except that the view is rather restricted! Here, a Petty Officer shows the modern facilities, with the depth gauge covered for security reasons. (HMS *Neptune*)

38. The most potent surface ships of the Royal Navy in the present decade are most certainly the light aircraft carriers of the *Invincible* Class. The second vessel to be commissioned was *Illustrious*, which was rushed through to completion in order to sail south and relieve her sister-ship *Invincible* on station off the Falkland Islands in September 1982. She is pictured here two years later during exercises in the English Channel, with Sea Kings embarked.

39. The major destroyers in service in the 1980s are the Type 42s, formerly called the *Sheffield* Class after the lead ship, sunk in the South Atlantic in May 1982. The Type 42s are area air defence ships, armed with the Sea Dart missile, the Vickers Mk. 8 gun, close-in 20mm and 30mm cannon and an embarked flight of one Lynx ASW/ASVW helicopter. Pictured here off Portland naval base, *Birmingham* was the second member of the class, commissioned on 3 December 1976.

▲40

40. Since commissioning in 1978 *Newcastle* (built by Swan Hunter) has been much travelled, visiting the South Atlantic even before the Falklands conflict. Like other units of the Batch 1 Type 42s, she is equipped with the large Type 965 radar which might nowadays be considered obsolescent. Following the Falklands War all the remaining Type 42s were fitted with close-range batteries of cannon and it is thought that they will eventually be fitted with a Close-In Weapon System (CIWS) such as Phalanx.

41. Five of the later Batch 3 *Leander*s have been extensively modified at Devonport in major refits which cost about £70 million. This work included the provision of Seawolf missiles, improved Type 2016 hull-mounted sonar, facilities to operate the Lynx, and modern STWS and electronic warfare (EW) systems. The Limbo mortar, 4.5in gun, Seacat missiles and Type 965 radar were removed.

42. The *Leander*s are the best-known postwar Royal Navy frigates. Originally completed as general-purpose warships, they have now been refitted for more specific roles. The Exocet variant is here illustrated by *Sirius* (F40), which was also one of the first in the class to embark a Lynx helicopter in place of the Wasp. *Leander*s have been exported to various friendly nations, and recently decommissioned RN frigates of the class have found their way south to the Royal New Zealand Navy.

43. *Danae* (F47), seen here leaving Portsmouth for a day of exercises in the English Channel, is one of the Exocet conversions in Batch 2 of the *Leander* Class. Built at the naval dockyard at Devonport, the frigate was launched in 1964 and commissioned three years later. The Exocet missiles give the ship an added over-the-horizon capability, but this weapon is becoming obsolete and must soon be replaced.

▼41

42▲   43▼

▲44

44. The Royal Navy's eight Type 21 frigates, ordered in 1968, represented the first commercial frigate design to be accepted for British service since the Second World War; they were also the first gas turbine-powered frigates in the RN. The first three were built by Vosper Thornycroft and the remaining five in Scotland by Yarrow, and the first Yarrow ship, *Ambuscade* (F172), is seen here off the Isle of Wight.

45. The Type 21 frigates brought new standards of accommodation to the Royal Navy and even in the 1980s they are still important warships: much of the post-Falklands criticism of their design was ill-founded, and the Admiralty has certainly not lost faith in the type. By 1985, all had been updated and fitted with Exocet, although it is doubtful whether they will receive a major mid-life refit. This is *Alacrity*, off Portland, showing the provision of SCOT (Satellite

Communications Terminals) either side of the funnel.

46. In dry dock at Portsmouth, an *Oberon* Class submarine shows her two stern torpedo tubes, which may be used to fire the free-running Mk. 8 torpedo; normally however, the forward tubes are used. The SSKs still have an important part to play in the Royal Navy's Submarine Flotilla, being quieter than nuclear boats and better suited to shallow-water work.

47. A member of the Third Submarine Squadron (SM3) at Faslane, *Walrus* is the oldest British submarine in commission as the Royal Navy reaches the middle of the 1980s. She was built as a *Porpoise* Class SSK and commissioned in 1961; since then refits have allowed her and her sisters to be brought up to the standard of the later *Oberon* Class, from which, externally, there is nothing to distinguish them. (HMS *Neptune*)

▼45

46▲ 47▼

29

▲48 ▼49

48. All submarines regularly operate with helicopters, especially in Scottish waters with 819 Sqn's Sea Kings based at Prestwick Airport. Here a passenger is being winched from *Oracle* (S16) aboard a Sea King HAS.2; he is wearing the orange 'once-only' immersion suit. The large dome on the forward casing of the submarine houses the sonar arrays, and note also the forward escape hatch and the radio mast on the fin top. (HMS *Gannet*)

49. The visit of Royal Navy warships to a coastal town or city allows the public to view the ships and their equipment at close hand. Here *Oracle* is pictured having just passed under Tower Bridge, her casing party preparing to make her fast to *Belfast*, the cruiser memorial ship in the Pool of London. Note that the forward planes are folded and

that flagstaffs are being positioned for ceremonial purposes. (RN)

50. At the end of a commission, a warship wears its paying-off pennant, the length of which is proportional to the length of the commission. It is usually flown from the highest point, which in the case of *Olympus* (S12) is the W/T mast. The boat is making her way up the Gare Loch to Faslane for a refit. (HMS *Neptune*)

51. Besides the Royal Navy, *Oberon* Class conventional submarines also equip the Commonwealth navies of Canada, Australia and New Zealand. The Australians have carried out a number of improvements, especially to the sonar fit, and it is interesting that the RN has copied the design of the sonar dome for a trial in *Opossum* (S19). (Mike Lennon).

▲52 ▼53

52. The *Leander*s were designed as improved Type 12 general-purpose frigates, armed with 4.5in Mk. 7 mountings, Seacat SAMs and a Westland Wasp HAS.1 helicopter. Over the last decade and a half, however, a number of the 26-strong class have been converted to more specialist roles; several others have been sold off. *Achilles* (F12) has the basic configuration of the class as built, although she is a Batch 3 vessel with a broader beam. Also in the photograph (which was taken off Australia) are *Aurora* (F10) and *Rothesay*, further Type 12s. (HMS *Invincible*)

53. The first major conversion was to the Batch 1 *Leander*s and involved replacing the 4.5in guns with the Anglo-Australian Ikara ASW system. Additional ASW weaponry includes the Mk. 10 Limbo ASW mortar aft and the Wasp helicopter; the latter can carry Mk. 44 and Mk. 46 ASW homing torpedoes to engage a submarine target at longer range. The Ikara air vehicle is launched from the gondola forward of the bridge and is guided via the bridge top director. Note also the 40mm Bofors guns on the bridge wings. (HMS *Osprey*)

54. One of the oldest *Leander*s remaining in service in the first half of the 1980s is *Ajax* (F114), seen here following a *County* Class destroyer into Gibraltar harbour after a NATO exercise. This view of the frigate shows the Wasp on the flight deck and the Limbo mortar tubes; the opening in the stern plates is for the variable-depth sonar, but several ships of the class had this facility converted into additional living space for the Royal Marines detachment. (CINCFLEET/RN)

55. In 1983, having been taken in hand for modification a second time, *Sirius* appeared with an enlarged starboard quarter, a towed array reel and fairlead and minus her ship's boats. To reduce topweight, the frigate lost her long-range Type 965 ('bedstead') search radar and forward Seacat launchers. The radar on the mainmast has been replaced by the Type 1006 navigation array. (Mike Lennon)

54▲   55▼

▲56

56, 57. The *Leander*
Class frigate *Phoebe*
(F42) was the star of the
1970s television series
Warship, and subsequent
series of the programme,
although shot with other
Leanders, maintained the
same pennant number.
In those days, *Phoebe*
was a conventional 'Gun
Leander', being con-
verted to take Exocet in
1974–77. By 1982, she
was sporting additional
20mm Oerlikon arma-
ment, on the bridge top
and quarterdeck, but
following the introduc-
tion of a towed array,
other modifications were
made. Having already
lost her ship's boats and
Type 965 radar, *Phoebe*
then lost her Oerlikons to
save topweight and to
make way for the towed
array reel. These two
views of the frigate
passing in and out of
Portsmouth harbour in
June 1984 show the
latest state of the *Leander*
art. (Mike Lennon)
58. *Argonaut* (F56),
damaged in Argentine
air attacks near San
Carlos, was a hero of the
South Atlantic
campaign. During her
subsequent refit and
repair at Devonport
Dockyard, it was decided
to fit her with the passive
ASW towed array. (P.O.
(Phot) Packenas/RN)

57▲ 58▼

59. All the *Leander* conversions have received the Plessey Marine Shipborne Torpedo Weapons System (STWS), although the Batch 2 vessels with towed array have had their triple sets moved a deck lower than *Cleopatra*'s original position. To the left of the tubes is the Corvus decoy and counter-measures launcher.

60. The Westland Wasp has now entered its third decade of service but is still embarked aboard the earlier *Leander*s and those of Batch 3 with gun armament. Although *Scylla* has been equipped with the Westland Lynx since this photograph was taken, the latter does illustrate the important features of the type – flotation gear, specially designed undercarriage for frigate-deck landings, sight for AS.12 anti-ship missiles and underfuselage attachment points for torpedoes and depth bombs. The crew comprises a pilot and gunner/crewman.

61. One of the earliest *Leander*s, *Penelope* (F127) had a most interesting career before her conversion to an 'Exocet *Leander*' in 1982. The ship was an original 'Gun *Leander*', but was taken in hand for conversion to a trials ship for the Seawolf guided missile system in 1971–73. Ironically, when she refitted in 1980–82 for Exocet, her surface-to-air missile fit reverted to Seacat, a generation older than Seawolf. (Plymouth/RN)

62. The 'Broad-Beamed *Leander*s' such as *Jupiter* (F60) differ from others of the class like *Danae* (F47, behind) in having 2ft more beam, which makes them more seaworthy and has allowed conversion for Seawolf and other advanced systems. It is possible that the earlier *Leander*s will be paid off during the late 1980s, but the Batch 3 frigates should remain in service for another ten years.

63. The Batch 3 *Leander* conversions (*Andromeda* is shown) are characterized by the prominent Seawolf launcher forward and four Exocet launchers. The Seawolf direction radar is on the bridge top, the ship's boats have been replaced by the Searider, twin SCOT communications aerials have appeared and the large Type 965 long-range air search radar has been removed to save topweight. The final recognition feature is the new funnel shape. (P.O. (Phot) Packenas/RN)

▲59 ▼60

◀64
65▲

64. This aerial bow shot of *Charybdis* – known as 'Cherry B' to the Fleet – shows the six Seawolf canisters to good advantage, as well as the low-set Exocets; the Type 910 Seawolf fire control radar on the bridge top and the mast-top Type 967/968 aerial are also well illustrated. The Batch 3 conversions have the older Corvus decoy launcher and the new Super RBOC system to launch chaff, flares and other decoy countermeasures against incoming missiles. (HMS *Osprey*)

65. The use of the towed array by British anti-submarine frigates has temporarily given the Western Alliance superiority over the submarine forces of potential enemies, in that the passive detection capability of the warships has been increased. *Cleopatra* (F28), although lacking ship's boats, is now well armed with Exocet forward, two 20mm Oerlikons, two Seacat quadruple launchers

(under cover on the hangar roof) and two triple STWS launchers abeam the hangar. The large towed array reel and the stern fairlead are clearly visible in this view of the the ship leaving Portsmouth. (Mike Lennon)

66. The immediate predecessors of the *Leander*s were the *Rothesay*s, or Modified Type 12 frigates, which were designed as specialist anti-submarine vessels. They did not originally carry the Wasp helicopter, but those remaining in service in the 1980s have all been fitted with the type. The ships acquitted themselves well in the Falklands conflict, especially in the role of gunnery support, using the forward-mounted 4.5in Mk. 7 gun and the bridge-top MRS.3 fire control director, as well as helicopters for aerial spotting. This is *Yarmouth*, seen entering Gibraltar. (RN)

66▼

▲67

67. *Falmouth* (F113) and her sister-ship *Plymouth* (F126) are destined to pay off in 1985–86, having come to the end of about twenty-five years of useful service. The latter, a veteran of the Falklands campaign will probably be scrapped, but the former, illustrated here, is due to become the Harbour Training Ship at Portsmouth. Note the cutaway quarterdeck, which is a useful distinguishing feature between the Modified Type 12s and their more modern *Leander* class semi-sisters. (HMS *Osprey*)

▼68

68. Having built the *Leander* Class as general-purpose frigates, the Admiralty wanted to replace the older specialist frigates with ships of an anti-submarine bias but still able to protect themselves from air and surface threats. For the first time since 1945 the RN turned to commercial designers, and the result was the Vosper Thornycroft Type 21 *Amazon* Class. The frigates were completed without Exocet, just having the then-new Vickers Mk. 8 4.5in gun, but by 1985 all six remaining Type 21s had been given an Exocet refit. (HMS *Neptune*)

69▲

69. The Type 21s were originally equipped with the Wasp, although they were designed to take the Lynx, but as more of the latter became available they were taken aboard. This is *Ambuscade* in June 1984, yet to receive Exocet but now fitted for (but not with) SCOT aerials and having STWS on 01 deck. Note the toned-down colours.

70. Despite some criticism during and after the South Atlantic campaign, the Type 21s are good surface combat ships. *Active* (F171) was the last to be built at Southampton by Vosper Thornycroft and is pictured here in completed form. Of interest are the Exocet launchers forward of the bridge and the ship's Wasp on the flight deck. (RN)

70▼

▲71

71. The Type 21s have been strengthened amidships as a result of their operations in the South Atlantic and elsewhere. The first of the Type to be so modified was *Arrow* (F173), seen here entering Portsmouth at the end of November 1984. The frigate wears her identification letters on the gaff – Sierra Romeo Juliet Sierra. (Mike Lennon)

72. Part of the RN's annual duties is the Group Deployment outside the NATO area. In 1980 *Avenger* (F185) was part of such a deployment, together with *Cleopatra* (F28) and *Amazon* (F169) seen in the background. The three frigates are shown leaving Devonport and the ship's companies are fallen in for leaving harbour. Of special interest are the SCOT domes on the superstructure, the STWS torpedo tubes and the embarked Lynx helicopter. (Plymouth Cmd./RN)

▼72

73. In the 1970s a fundamental change was made in the design of British frigates – a change that was proved to be ill-conceived following the actions in the South Atlantic. The Type 22 frigates, which will continue to be built throughout the 1980s, were the first of their type to dispense with a main gun armament, employing the Exocet missile in its stead; they were also the first warships to carry the Seawolf SAM. (Fleet Photographic Unit)

74. Powered by gas turbine engines, the Type 22 or *Broadsword* Class frigates are proving to be a tremendous asset to the RN and, although designed for anti-submarine escort and patrol work, the later Batches have more of a general-purpose capability. This view of *Broadsword* at speed illustrates the two Seawolf launchers and the unusual funnel arrangement. (HMS *Osprey*)

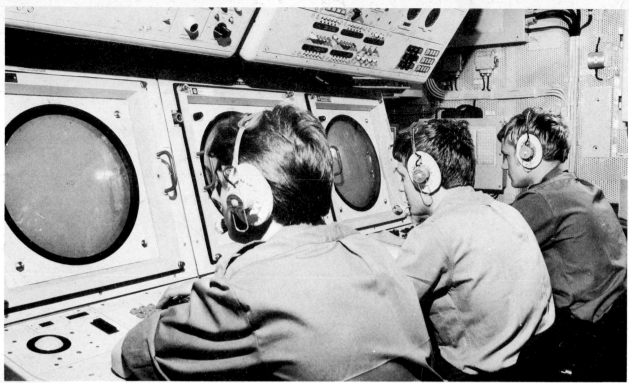

 ▲75   ▼76

75. The main anti-submarine sensor of the Type 22s is the Type 2016 Fleet Escort Sonar, part of the Action Information Organization. In battle, the operators would be dressed for 'action' in anti-flash gear, and the environment of the Operations Room would be dimmed and specially lit. (Plessey Marine)

76. The main anti-aircraft defence for the *Broadswords* is provided by the Seawolf short-range guided missile; one is seen here leaving *Battleaxe*'s forward launcher. The Seawolf has been proven in combat, accounting for five aircraft in the Falklands campaign. In addition, trials have confirmed its capability against subsonic, supersonic and sea-skimming missile targets, as well as against 4.5in shells. (British Aerospace)

77. Just after this photograph of *Ambuscade* was taken in the English Channel the frigate commenced her 15-month refit to receive surface-to-surface missiles. The Exocet refit commenced in October 1984 and the opportunity was taken to stiffen the hull in order to improve seaworthiness, as in the other five surviving ships of the class.

78. The Northern Flank of NATO, the Atlantic Alliance, is one of the areas most vulnerable to enemy ingress. Every year, units of the Royal Navy operate with the Royal Norwegian Navy in joint exercises designed to test readiness and team-work. In 1983, the name-ship of the Type 21 frigates, *Amazon*, sailed as escort to a group of merchant ships carrying Royal Marine Commandos, and she is pictured here in the midday sun, north of the Arctic Circle.

79. ▲79 ▼80

79. At the end of 1982 the ice patrol ship *Endurance* was due to pay off, but the actions of the Argentines ensured that she would remain in service during the 1980s. The ship is pictured here off South Georgia in June 1982, following the liberation of this southerly island by the Royal Navy. *Endurance*'s role as an ice patrol ship includes scientific research, 'flag showing' and deterrence. She is equipped with two Westland Wasp HAS.1 helicopters, both of which were in action against the Argentine submarine *Santa Fe* in 1982. (RN)

80. For special roles connected with the Royal Marines, the RN has two landing ships, which also serve as 'flag showers' and occasionally as Dartmouth Training Ships for naval officer cadets; in wartime their role would be to support operations in NATO flank areas, particularly Norway. This is *Fearless*, photographed during Exercise 'Cold Winter' in 1983, on passage in the Inner Leads. A replacement for these ships is urgently required in order to ensure that the Royals keep their capability.

81. The importance of carrying out replenishment at sea is also stressed by the Royal Navy in the 1980s. Many observers consider the RN to be masters of the art, but such operations are not always undertaken in the perfect conditions shown here. In the foreground is *Cleopatra*, performing a jackstay transfer, and in the distance a stores support ship and two frigates RAS (replenish-at-sea). The helicopter hovering above the RFA's stern is a Fleet Air Arm Wessex HU.5, demonstrating Vertrep (vertical replenishment).

82. An important fact, highlighted by the Falklands campaign, is that the Royal Navy sails courtesy of the Royal Fleet Auxiliary (RFA): without the tankers, stores ships and ammunition carriers, the modern warship would be hard put to remain at sea for very long, and during any naval exercise or operation the RFAs will not be far behind, Here, off Norway, RFA *Appleleaf* is about to begin a replenishment of *Hermes*.

▲83 ▼84

85▲

83. Part of the ever-growing threat to the freedom of the seas is the mine, and mine warfare is an important aspect of the Royal Navy's work. NATO co-operation is very important, as shown here by the presence of the Belgian mines countermeasures vessel *Breydel* (right) at the RN's Mine Warfare Establishment at *Vernon*, Portsmouth. The other ship is the glassfibre-hull experimental vessel HMS *Wilton*.
84. The *Ton* Class minesweepers were built in the 1950s, and several were converted for patrol duties in the Persian Gulf and the South China Sea. In the 1980s the five remaining craft in Hong Kong will be replaced by new vessels, but here are *Monkton* (foreground) and *Beachampton* leaving *Tamar*, the Hong Kong naval establishment, for a routine patrol around the 600-plus islands of the colony. Their duties include anti-smuggling and anti-piracy patrols.

85. In the light of the Falklands experience, the Type 22s have also been toned down in colour: *Brilliant*, a veteran of the 1982 campaign (especially the recapture of South Georgia) illustrates the overall grey. The pennant number is also normally toned down, or even removed altogether. (Mike Lennon)
86. The *Broadswords* were the first frigates in the RN to be designed to metric tolerances, and the first to be equipped to operate two Lynx helicopters, kept in the double hangar. However, the protracted delivery of the Lynx has meant that the ships have been complemented for a single helicopter until the order has been completed by Westland. This is *Brilliant* again, making way astern. (HMS *Dolphin*)

86▼

▲87 ▼88

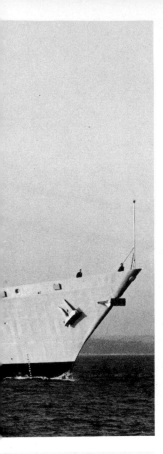

87. In a similar move to that undertaken with the Type 42 guided missile destroyers, the second batch of four Type 22 frigates have been lengthened. Still retaining the rakish profile, the Batch 2 ships have a new funnel arrangement, a longer bridge structure and a sharper, clipper bow. There is no port anchor, to avoid damage to the repositioned Type 2016 sonar dome under the waterline. This is *Boxer* (F92) on delivery to Plymouth in September 1984. (Mike Lennon)

88. *Boxer* is the first of the Type 22 Batch 2s to embark a ship's flight of two Lynx from 815 Sqn.; a sister-ship, *Brave* (F94), will have a strengthened and lengthened stern to accommodate the first EH.101 (Sea King replacement) helicopters in the late 1980s. In this view of *Boxer*, she is fitted for but not with SCOT and also has had her ship's boats removed. (Mike Lennon)

89. Six Types 22s had been commissioned by the beginning of 1985, including the second Batch 2 vessel, *Beaver* (F93), built at the Yarrow yard on the Clyde. This photograph, taken during the frigate's sea trials, shows off the Exocet and Seawolf missile systems as well as the modern radar, countermeasures and electronic warfare suites. The ships are capable of at least 30kts, or 18kts when cruising on their Tynes alone. (Yarrow)

90. Replacing the frigates in the Economic Zone patrols are the offshore patrol vessels, such as the specially designed *Castle* Class, of which *Leeds Castle* (P258) was the first to commission. Although not embarking its own helicopter, *Leeds Castle* is helicopter-capable and has good endurance. The role of the OPV is to patrol the important fishing and natural resource areas, including the North Sea. (FOSNI/RN)

▲91 ▼92

91. The 1980s see three
types of OPV in service:
the *Ton* Class have been
adapted from coastal
minesweepers (*Wotton* is
illustrated, foreground);
the *Islands* are based on a
Fisheries Protection
design first used for the
Scottish Agriculture and
Fisheries Service
(*Anglesey*, centre); and
the third vessel is *Leeds
Castle*. The Fisheries
Protection Squadron is
based at Rosyth in
Scotland but operates
around the coastal and
offshore waters of the
entire United Kingdom.
(FOSNI/RN)
92. *Island* Class craft,
like *Shetland*, are lightly
armed, having only
general-purpose machine
guns (GPMGs) and a
single Bofors 40mm gun
mounting (forward of the
bridge). Their main role
is to stop and inspect
fishing craft, patrol the
offshore oil and gas platforms and provide a
general protection
service. *Shetland* wears
the Fisheries Protection
yellow and blue
chequered pennant on
her funnel. (FOSNI/RN)
93. Rosyth has an
important role, con-
venient as it is for the
North Sea and
Norwegian Sea areas. In
order to provide a full
maintenance and repair
service, a synchro-lift
was commissioned in the
early 1980s to take the
Offshore Patrol Vessels
out of the water and into
a covered maintenance
area. In this photograph
Orkney (P299) is being
prepared for re-
launching. (FOSNI/RN)
93▶

▲94

▲95 ▼96

94. An earlier experiment to produce a small, cost-effective offshore patrol craft was not wholly successful, and the *Bird* Class are now used for navigational training and patrol work within Flag Officer Scotland and Northern Ireland's domain. This beautiful shot of *Cygnet* (P261) was taken off Portland by the Photographic Section at HMS *Osprey* during the ship's work-up. (RN)

95. Besides being adapted for offshore patrol duties in United Kingdom waters, the *Ton* Class craft have for some years been operating out of Hong Kong. The Hong Kong Patrol, of which *Monkton* (P1055) was half-leader in 1981, operated five during the early 1980s. They have been modified to carry two 40mm guns and pintle-mounted GPMGs and have had their sweep gear removed.

96. Shown here testing the Victoria Harbour typhoon moorings, *Wasperton* (P1089) wears the broad funnel cap of the Squadron Leader and also displays the Squadron's funnel badge and the Type 1006 navigation radar which is also used for surveillance. The *Ton*s are used in Colony waters to assist the Royal Hong Kong Police maritime units guard against smugglers and illegal immigrants.

97. As the *Ton*s are now all rather long in the tooth, the Royal Navy, in co-operation with the Colony's government, has commissioned the design and building of a new class from Hall Russell in Aberdeen. The first craft arrived in the Colony in the autumn of 1984, a year after the third craft, *Starling* (P241, shown) was launched. Note the dual-purpose OTO-Melara 76mm gun mounting, giving the *Peacock* Class considerable 'teeth'.

98. Scheduled to be paid off but reprieved because of the Falklands conflict, the RN's ice patrol ship *Endurance* was initially the only British 'warship' in the South Atlantic in 1982. Fitted for ocean survey work (hence the survey launches on special davits) and carrying two Westland Wasp helicopters, the ship was purchased from the Danes in 1967 for work in that region. *Endurance* is painted in bright red and is unarmed when operating in Antarctic Treaty waters. (FOSNI/RN)

99. The need to move the men and equipment of the Royal Marines to Norway and other flank areas in time of tension is borne by the assault ships *Fearless* (illustrated) and *Intrepid*. The LPDs have a docking well aft, under the flight deck, which accommodates four LCUs, and there are a similar number of LCVPs on the davits. There is no accommodation for helicopters, which have to be parked on deck.

97 ▲

98 ▲ 99 ▼

▲100 ▼101

K07

100. Part-way between a landing ship and a helicopter carrier is RFA *Reliant*, seen here prior to operations off the Lebanon in January 1984. *Reliant* is a converted container ship which carries a special decking and hangar facilities for the operation of helicopters; note the Westland Wessex HU.5 keeping station to port. No defensive armament can be seen in this photograph, but the ship does carry countermeasures launchers. (HMS *Osprey*)

101, 102, 103. One of the most interesting naval vessels to joint the RN in the 1980s is the Diving Support Ship *Challenger*. At 7,200 tons she is the fifth largest vessel sailing under the White Ensign, and she has been equipped for many types of specialist diving, as well as with a flight deck and heavy-duty cranes. The saturation diving bell is lowered through the centre of the ship and there is also a special lifting derrick aft. One of a kind, *Challenger* (K07) cost over £80 million to build and in photograph 103 is seen demonstrating her dynamic positioning system. (Mike Lennon)

102▲ 103▼

▲104

104. Home of the Fisheries Protection craft, certain frigates and destroyers, and also operating as a submarine refit facility, Rosyth is now the only naval base on the British east coast. Seen here during a Navy Day celebration, the base is welcoming British and other NATO naval vessels. In the foreground, on the camera's side of the wharf, is *Abdiel* (N21), a minesweeper depot ship and former net-layer. Immediately behind are two *County* Class destroyers which were paid off in the 1980s, *Antrim* (nearest) and *London*. The latter's name is being taken by a Type 22 frigate in 1986. (FOSNI/RN)

105. The recent reawakening to the threat of mines in British and NATO waters prompted the development of a high-technology mines countermeasures vessel (MCMV) known as the *Hunt* Class. These vessels are constructed of glass-reinforced fibre materials, and are capable of both minehunting and minesweeping. The craft displace 725 tons, and at least twelve will enter service in the 1980s, most being built by Vosper Thornycroft. This is *Ledbury* (M30), the second of the class to be commissioned. (VT)

▼105

106. In 1982 *Ledbury* and *Brecon* were called upon to operate around the Falkland Islands to clear Argentine mines and explosives – the first opportunity for *Hunt* class craft to experience 'live' conditions and demonstrate their abilities. In this photograph the craft are seen taking fuel and water from the support ship RMS *St. Helena*. (*Wind Jammer* via VT)

107. To provide the Royal Naval Reserve (RNR) with additional vessels for their wartime MCM role, and partly to replace the ageing *Tons*, the RN has ordered a number of *River* Class minesweepers; *Waveney* (M2003) is depicted departing Portsmouth in June 1984. The craft has been alongside at *Vernon*, the RN's Mine Warfare Establishment which is due to close in 1986 as a result of recent defence economies. (Mike Lennon)

107 ▼

▲108 ▼109

108. Three *Ton* Class MCMVs of the 10th MCM Squadron, RNR, operating together off Gibraltar. All are rated as coastal minesweepers (as identified by the their floats and boards), and all are armed with the 40mm Bofors gun. The craft are, from camera to horizon, *Cuxton* (M1125), *Wotton* (M1195) and *Shavington* (M1180). These vessels are made of laminated wooden and low-ferrous materials. (FOSNI/RN)

109. *Shavington* illustrates the tackle and equipment used in mine-sweeping, the principles of which have not changed since the First World War. Manned by the mainly part-time members of the RNR, the craft are cost-effective assets to the Fleet. (FOSNI/RN)

110. The main defensive armament of the *Ton*s is the 40mm Bofors gun, which can be supplemented by pintle-mounted GPMGs. Also aboard are a number of small arms for use in the detonation of mines which surface after having been cut loose by the sweep wires. *Cuxton* (shown) is fitted with Kelvin-Hughes Type 1006 navigation radar. (FOSNI/RN)

111. The diminutive size and interesting construction of the *Ton* class are illustrated in this view of the minehunter *Brereton* (M1113) in one of the large dry docks at Gibraltar. (RN)

110▲ 111▼

▲112 ▼113

62

114▲

112. First commissioned in 1955, *Kellington* (M1154) was converted for the role of specialist minehunter and has spent much of the 1980s as an RNR training tender operating with the 10th MCM Squadron. Various marker and mine warfare equipment can be seen on deck, as well as two Gemini rubber boats used for taking divers to a point over a possible mine on the seabed. For self-protection, *Kellington* is armed with the standard 40mm Bofors on the foredeck. (FOSNI/RN)

113. To provide British and NATO frigates and other escorts with replenishment at sea, a class of five small tankers were commissioned in the early 1970s. The *Rover* Class play an important part in exercises and routine patrols and were, of course, present during the South Atlantic campaign. This is *Grey Rover* (A269), first of the class; all were built on the Tyne by Swan Hunter. Note the SCOT radome and the helicopter deck aft.

114. One of the specialist 'out of area' deployments which has been a regular aspect of RN life since 1980 is the Gulf Protection Patrol, which is part of the international effort to assist neutral shipping during the protracted Iraq-Iran war; as part of the patrol, at least two British escorts, with their replenishment support tanker, are to be found in the Gulf of Oman. In this photograph, taken in early 1984, the RFA tanker *Blue Rover* is refuelling-at-sea ('rasing') the Union Flag-bedecked Type 22 frigate *Brazen* (left) and the Type 12 frigate *Rothesay*. After this Gulf Patrol *Brazen* returned to the UK and was joined by Lt. HRH Prince Andrew as the ship's flight's pilot. (RN)

115. Royal Fleet Auxiliaries, although registered as merchantmen, are fully integrated into the Royal Navy: they are either owned by the Ministry of Defence or, in the case of some bulk oilers, under contract. During the year, various evaluations are carried out which might be useful in time of war. During 'Autumn Train 1984', the aircraft carrier *Illustrious* took the fleet oiler *Olmeda* in tow. On the carrier's deck are Sea Harrier FRS.1s from 800 Sqn. and a single Sea King HAS.5 from 814 Sqn. (HMS *Illustrious*)

◄115

118▲

116–119. Carrying out a replenishment underway requires considerable skill and experience for all concerned. To illustrate the replenishment of a Type 42's Sea Dart magazine from the special stores ship *Resource* (A480), the following sequence will be of interest. Initially, the stores ship steers a set course, into wind if possible, and the receiving warship closes from astern. Once stabilized alongside, the warship sends across lines, including a guide to indicate distance (116); from here, the helm order is 'nothing to starboard'. With the initial lines across, both vessels rig special jackstays to begin the transfer. The Sea Dart missiles, enclosed in canisters, are guided by seamen on both ships (117) and, for the purposes of this English Channel exercise between *Resource* and *Manchester*, returned to the RFA again (118). Once the RAS has been completed, the warship will accelerate away – in the case of vessels fitted with gas turbine engines, this manoeuvre can be very spectacular (119)!

119▼

▲120 ▼121

122 ▲

120. 'Autumn Train' was interesting exercise involving the use of two small carrier task groups, based around *Illustrious* (distance) and *Invincible*. From left to right, other warships visible here are PNS *Corrba*; *Jupiter* and *Tidespring* (with *Invincible*); *Fort Grange*; *Alacrity*; *Berwick* and *Olmeda* (with *Illustrious*); and *Cleopatra* leading *Manchester*. (HMS *Illustrious*)

121. An aim for the 1990s is to produce a 'one-stop' replenishment vessel for the Royal Navy which would not only be armed for self-defence but also have provision for helicopters; a step in that direction was the building of the two *Fort* Class fleet replenishment ships, which commissioned in the late 1970s. With a displacement of 22,800 tons, the *Forts*, which both served in the South Atlantic, can carry four Sea Kings and mount 20mm Oerlikon self-defence weapons. (Scott-Lithgow)

122. The Royal Yacht *Britannia* passes the RFA's tank farm and oiling berths at Gosport. This magnificent symbol of British naval pride was designed for conversion into a hospital ship in time of war, but was not used as such during the limited conflict in the South Atlantic when merchantmen such as cruise ships were taken up from trade and survey ships suitably converted. *Britannia* has a ship's company of 21 officers and 256 ratings, all specially chosen, and the ship, normally berthed at *Excellent* in Portsmouth Harbour, costs a little over £2 million a year to run. (L.A. (Phot) Dales/RN)

123. A special service provided to the world by the RN is the Admiralty Chart, prepared primarily for naval use but available also to the general public. The largest of the ships in the Survey Flotilla are the *Hecla* and *Herald* Classes, totalling four ocean-going ships. These vessels are fitted with the most modern equipment, including satellite navigation control, computerized plotting, gravimeters, magnetometers, echo-sounders and special survey boats. The importance of modern oceanography, especially to anti-submarine warfare, is to be judged by the fact that the Survey Service is expanding. This is the most recent ocean-going survey ship, *Herald* (A138).

123 ▼

▲124 ▼125

126▲

124. The bridge plot of a survey ship on task. The photograph appears to have been taken immediately after a sun sight at noon and the captain (a Commander RN) is calculating the ship's position. Even with modern satellite aids, the Royal Navy still practises the basic skills of navigation. The survey ships have bridge control for steering and engine orders. (RN)

125. For coastal work at home and abroad the RN has a class of four 1,088-ton ships, with a fifth on order from Brooke Marine. The *Bulldog* Class, although designed for work in the Caribbean and Persian Gulf, now operate, in pairs, in the waters around the UK's natural resource exploitation platforms and major shipping routes. The ships have been completed to commercial rather than to naval standards, are unarmed, and are generally painted white and buff.

126. In addition to the Royal Fleet Auxiliary Service, the RN has the benefit of the Royal Maritime Auxiliary Service, a civilian organization which provides specialist craft for naval purposes, for example four torpedo recovery craft for trials and operational training. This is the Hall Russell-built *Torch* (A141), which is based at Portland and carries out work for the Admiralty Underwater Weapons Establishment. (British Shipbuilders)

127. *Lodestone* (A115) is a specialist degaussing vessel based at Portsmouth and charged, in wartime, with the role of attending to the magnetic properties of vessels and their protection against magnetic mines. The 955-ton ship was launched in 1979 and has a sister-ship operating in the Clyde area. (HMS *Dolphin*)

127▼

▲128

128. The ocean-going tug has many uses in the RN, including the towing of naval and auxiliary craft that have paid off and been sold for scrapping. Seen leaving Portsmouth in 1982 is the ocean tug *Roysterer* (A361), with the former paddlewheel tug *Forceful* in tow for the breakers. The latter's name has now been taken by a new twin-unit tractor class vessel due to enter service in the late 1980s. *Roysterer* has a rated bollard pull of 50 tons and was specially designed for long-range salvage and towing work. (HMS *Dolphin*)

129. Some of the older tugs are being paid off in the 1980s, including the remaining units of the *Confiance* Class, which now includes the three *Agile* Class vessels. *Agile*, pictured here entering Portsmouth Harbour and passing the submarine school *Dolphin*, was originally based at Gibraltar, but returned home on that dockyard's closure. *Agile* was built by Goole Shipbuilders in 1959. (Portsmouth/RN)

▼129

130. Designed to replace the *Confiance* Class, the four twin-unit tractors of the *Adept* Class are designed primarily for coastal and harbour work and possess great manoeuvrability. *Adept* operates out of Portsmouth and is pictured here with that base's semaphore tower in the background and the *County* Class guided missile destroyer *Glamorgan* alongside. Note the provision of fire-fighting equipment. (RN)

131. The *Girl* Class harbour berthing tugs are frequent sights around British naval ports and dockyards. *Dorothy* (A173) is based at Portsmouth (she is pictured in 1978 when the cruiser *Blake*, background, was still in commission), but others have served in Hong Kong and Gibraltar. Built by Dunstons and completed in 1972, the tug has a gross tonnage of 38 and sees constant service in the harbour. (Tony Wilson/RN)

132. It is the smaller naval and auxiliary craft which, although not often in the limelight, make the harbours, ports and dockyards 'tick'. Stores and personnel are transferred around Portland, for example, by fleet tenders like *Holmwood*, which is shown here serving the stores ship *Regent*, laying on a buoy in Portland Harbour. There are over thirty fleet tenders available to the RMAS and some have very specialist roles, even operating with the Royal Marines.

133. The Royal Naval Auxiliary Service operates craft for the RN and in time of war would no doubt be involved in harbour patrols and channel guides, and although its craft are dated it performs a vital task. *Portisham* is seen here giving visitors to the Portsmouth Navy Days a 'taste of the salt'. The fact that there is an RNXS means that naval and naval reserve personnel can undertake military-oriented roles.

▲132 ▼133